How to be Twittertastic

A Writers and Authors Guide to Twitter

By Jo Linsdell

Disclosure: This book is in no way sponsored or endorsed by Twitter and has no direct association with the company.

First published: July 2014

ASIN: B00LFFRYEE
First print version published: May 2015
ISBN-13: 978-1512051766

ISBN-10: 1512051764

www.JoLinsdell.com

About the Author

"Jo is one of those rare writers who really "gets" not only the art of writing but the business and promotional sides as well. In addition to her books and e-books, she's done a great service for the writing community through her Promo Day efforts, and anyone taking her on in a writing or editorial capacity would certainly benefit from her practical knowledge and experience in that area."

Jennifer Mattern, *Owner, JH Mattern Communications*

Jo Linsdell is the author of Six books, including; *Virtual Book Tours: Effective Online Book Promotion From the Comfort of Your Own Home, Italian for Tourists, A Guide to Weddings in Italy, Out and About at the Zoo, Fairy May* and *The Box*. Most of which have been international best sellers. She is also the illustrator of the *A Birthday Clown for Archer* series (written by Kathy Mashburn) and the *Jasmine Dreams* series (written by Maria Rochelle).

She is the founder and CEO of Writers and Authors and Promo Day. Linsdell studied A-levels in Business Studies, History and Art and has won several awards in her career. She was named the *Who's Who in the writing industry* in 2009.

Contents

Preface

"Social media is not just an activity; it is an investment of valuable time and resources. Surround yourself with people who not just support you and stay with you, but inform your thinking about ways to WOW your online presence"

@2morrowknight

Social media is a blur of tweets, shares, and content. It is worldwide and embedded in every corner of the internet. According to SEJ (Search Engine Journal) 72% of all internet users are now active on social media and a whooping 71% of users access social media from a mobile device.

In the **Writers and Authors Guide to Social Media** series I'll be taking you through the "how to" of the top sites and sharing tips and strategies to help you leverage your social media activity to build your author brand and sell more books.

Twitter is the most immediate of all social media and a real powerhouse to have in your corner. As of 2014, the site boasts over 1 billion users and plays a key role in news distribution, major events worldwide, and, of course, networking and marketing.

In this book you'll learn how to set up your account and personalise your profile for maximum impact as well as tips and strategies to help you get the most out of your Twitter efforts.

Section 1: What is Twitter?

What is Twitter: Chapter 1

The creation of Twitter

"#Twitter is a place where one person can help another person anywhere in the world."

@TweetSmarter

Before we jump into the how to part of this book I thought it would be a good idea to cover exactly what Twitter is. The reason being that each social media platform is different and should therefore be used in different ways. By understanding the idea behind Twitter and how it has developed you will have a better idea of Twitter mentality and be able to insert yourself into the Twitterverse with more ease.

How it began

Twitter was launched 21st March 2006 by creators Jack Dorsey, Biz Stone, Evan Williams, and Noah Glass when Dorsey published the first Twitter message at 9:50 PM Pacific Standard Time (PST).

What Is Twitter?

The first ever Tweet

Twitter was unlike any of the other social networks and, as the concept was so new, the company didn't even know where it was going at the start. It has evolved over time and is now one of the most powerful sites on the internet.

The name "Twitter" means 'a short burst of inconsequential information,' and 'chirps from birds'. And that's exactly what the product was.

It didn't take long for Twitter to take off. The company experienced rapid growth and was soon one of the top social networking sites on the internet. As of 2014, Twitter has over 1 billion total users, 255 million of which are active users sending out over 500 million tweets each and every day.

Since 2012 the symbol of Twitter has been the "Larry Bird" (which replaced the text "twitter" and the lower case "t" that had been previously used). The bird is now the sole symbol of the company's branding.

The "Larry Bird"

What is Twitter: Chapter 2

What is Twitter?

"Twitter is not a technology. It's a conversation. And it's happening with or without you."

@charleneli

So what is Twitter?

Twitter is microblogging. Twitter is social media. Twitter is an information network. Twitter is the SMS of the internet. Twitter is a highly powerful tool you can use to market your books and build your author brand... completely free of charge.

Twitter is an information network made up of 140 character status updates known as "Tweets". Whilst at first you might think this bullet sized posting format would be limiting, once you dive into Twitter you'll soon find that that is the beauty of the site and exactly why it's such a great social media site for busy writers and authors.

At the mere mention of marketing many authors respond that they don't have time to be active on social media. Time spent writing blog posts and creating or finding content worthy of sharing takes away too much time from the writing of books. I think you'll all agree that 140 characters isn't going to eat away at too much of your writing time.

In the Twitterverse you can say a quick hello to a writing colleague, share a photo of you slaving away on your current work in progress, and much more in the matter of seconds. I'll be covering more about the types of content you can share later on in chapter 9 so I won't go into that too much now. The point is that Twitter is much lower maintenance than most other social media sites and yet pulls in some of the best results for ROI (return on investment).

If you use the mobile version on your smartphone or tablet you can take it everywhere with you too. I personally use the mobile version on my phone when taking a writing break so I don't get too distracted by the internet in general. On my laptop I find it so easy to hop on for a quick check in and end up surfing around for hours. On my phone it's easier to limit myself to a retweet or two. It's also great to fill time whilst waiting around for the kettle to boil. A frequent online presence without being glued to the site all day long. I'll be taking a closer look at mobile Twitter and how you can use it later on in chapter 13.

Twitter is up to the minute and enables quick reactions. It facilitates word of mouth and viral sharing and makes it easy to track your competitors/hot topics in your niche. A minimal effort, high output marketing channel that's available to all writers and authors completely free of charge. Simply put, Twitter is one social media site you can't and shouldn't ignore.

Section 2: Getting started

Getting started: Chapter 3

Creating an account

"Social media is here. It's not going away; not a passing fad. Be where your customers are: in social media."

@loriruff

Setting up your profile

In this chapter I'm going to take you through the step by step of setting up your profile and optimising it for best results. Before we jump into the how to of setting up your Twitter account, there are a few things you need to consider.

Think about SEO

Social media and SEO (Search Engine Optimisation) compliment each other and therefore by optimising your Twitter account you can take advantage of this to improve your social footprint.

Picking a username

When you set up your Twitter account you can choose what

name you use. One way to help your account show up in searches for authors is to include "author" as a keyword in your account name.

Here's a example of how others are doing this:

Author Sylvia Day uses her name followed by a dot (for separation and easy reading) and "Author".

Picking a Twitter handle

Pick a Twitter handle that has your main keyword in it. As authors, this will usually be your penname as that is your author brand. Alternatively you could use the name of your book or even set up a Twitter account under the name of one of your characters and Tweet as them.

Here's an example of how others are including the keyword "Author" in their Twitter handle:

Author Dan Brown puts the word "Author" in front of his name.

In this example author Khalid Muhammad uses his name as his username and the name of his book series in his Twitter handle:

Here's an example of an account set up to tweet as the character from a book:

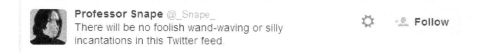

This account is set up in the name of Professor Snape from the Harry Potter series and the tweets shared on the account are all from his point of view.

You can, of course, set up more than one account. You could use one to tweet under your author brand and another to tweet as a character from your book. I suggest starting with just an author brand account first though and then adding more accounts later once you're more experienced using Twitter.

Now we've covered usernames and Twitter handles you're ready to sign up and set up your account.

Creating Your Account

When you go to www.Twitter.com you're presented with this page:

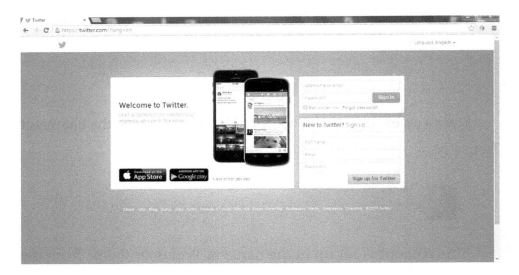

Fill out the sections in the "New to Twitter?" box and click the "Sign up for Twitter" button.

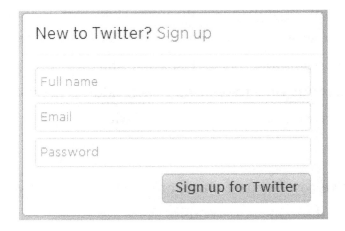

You'll then be taken to this page where you can complete the sign up and create your account:

Join Twitter today.

Full name

Enter your first and last name.

Email address

Create a password

Choose your username

☑ Keep me signed-in on this computer.

By clicking the button, you agree to the terms below:

These Terms of Service ("**Terms**") govern your access to and use of the services, including our various websites, SMS, APIs, email notifications.

Printable versions:
Terms of Service · Privacy Policy · Cookie Use

Create my account

Note: Others will be able to find you by name, username or email. Your email will not be shown publicly. You can change your privacy settings at any time.

Getting started: Chapter 4

Personalising your account

" #TwitterTip - add a profile picture or a logo, "eggheads" scream #newbie to all who see your account"

@InSouthFlorida

Getting personal

With over 1 billion registered users you want to make sure your profile grabs the attention of potential readers. One way of doing this is to personalise your profile. In this chapter I'll cover how to personalise your profile to strengthen your author brand.

On 22nd April 2014, Twitter released its new design (the biggest ever makeover the site has ever seen) and radically changed the site structure. The reason for the change was to give more importance to images and buttons and make it more like the experience you get with mobile devices.

So how can you personalise your profile?

Your profile avatar

Personalizing Your Account

Twitter automatically gives you an "egghead" as your profile avatar in keeping with their bird theme. Egghead accounts aren't taken seriously on Twitter especially as the majority of profiles showing them are spam accounts. You therefore want to make sure you upload an avatar to represent you on site and show you're a real person.

In the new twitter design, launched April 2014, the size of the profile picture is 400 x 400 pixels.

Your profile avatar will show up next to all of your tweets on the newsfeed so aim for a clutter-free, clear, image that will look good in the tiny thumbnail.

Think about your author branding. If using a photo of yourself, try to use the same author photo across all of your social media sites so you are easily recognisable to your fans.

Obviously the image you use will depend of the type of profile you have created. For author accounts you'll probably use your official author photo. An account for a specific book might use the book logo. If your book has been made into a film and you're using your account as a character from your book, use a photo of the actor/actress that plays the character in the costume from the film. You get the idea.

Your header photo

Twitter now gives you a huge space at the top of your profile dedicated to your profile header photo and, unlike some of the other social media sites, there are currently no rules about including text and links on it. This gives you a billboard to show who you are and promote your books.

Here's a screenshot of my Twitter profile:

As you can see I've used the header banner to showcase some of my books, included my website url, and a call to action to promote my illustration services. The blue background tones in with my website colours and I've used my official author photo for my profile avatar.

The size of the banner image is 1500 x 500 pixels.

Your bio

You'll also notice in the screenshot above the small section just below the avatar. This is where your bio is featured.

You're given up to 160 characters for your bio and so need to use them wisely. You'll want to make sure you include your keywords to help with SEO ranking both on site and in off site search engines.

In mine I list my main roles but end it with a more personal touch. I confess to being a "social media junky" which allows me to put in more keywords whilst at the same time giving some insight into me as a person.

I also added a little heart right at the end. Why the heart? Because it's a bit different. Not everyone is using emoticons in their bio's and so it stands out. It also gives it a personal touch and clearly shows I'm a real person and not an auto bot account. It gives my bio more personality and shows my fun side.

Your link

Right below the bio you have a space for inserting your location and a url of your choice. As you only have space for one link here I suggest either using your author website url or your author/sales page for your books.

When people click on your name in the newsfeed they get a "Profile summary " in which they can view your most recent tweets. They can then select to view your full profile.

In this example you can see how the author Terry Tyler uses the bio area to add the link to her blog and then inserts her Amazon author page as her chosen link.

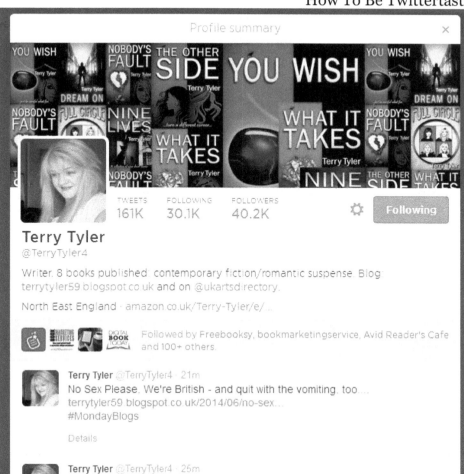

Profile summary   ×

TWEETS   FOLLOWING   FOLLOWERS
161K   30.1K   40.2K   ⚙   Following

Terry Tyler
@TerryTyler4

Writer. 8 books published: contemporary fiction/romantic suspense. Blog:
terrytyler59.blogspot.co.uk and on @ukartsdirectory.

North East England · amazon.co.uk/Terry-Tyler/e/...

Followed by Freebooksy, bookmarketingservice, Avid Reader's Cafe
and 100+ others.

Terry Tyler @TerryTyler4 · 21m
No Sex Please, We're British - and quit with the vomiting, too....
terrytyler59.blogspot.co.uk/2014/06/no-sex...
#MondayBlogs

Details

Terry Tyler @TerryTyler4 · 25m
@writingmind Hi Nicki, not seen you for ages! Hope you're okay x

Personalizing Your Account
In summary, you should have;

- An avatar

- A profile header banner

- A bio containing keywords

- Your main link(s)

- Be professional but show your personality.

Section 3: Creating your network

Creating your network: Chapter 5

Building your following

" Twitter is fun because it lets me stay in touch with all my original readers who grew up with my books"

Benefits of growing your following

You'll probably have heard people saying it's important to grow your following. As all tweets on Twitter are public you may wonder why it's such a big deal.

Let's take a look at why it's important to grow your following on Twitter.

Increases brand awareness.

Twitter is great for letting people know who you are. As an author, your brand is you. By using Twitter to demonstrate your expertise in your niche you can become known as an expert and attract potential customers. You create your brand by sharing your ideas, your passions, and your work.

Distributes your content to a wider audience.

When people follow you on Twitter your tweets show up in their

35

newsfeed. More people following you means more people that will see your tweets in their newsfeed.

Drives traffic to your website, blog, and/or sales page.

Twitter improves link building to your website and therefore improves your organic SEO.

Ways you can grow your following

Before we go any further you need to know something very important about growing your Twitter following. There are literally thousands of GFF (Get Followers Fast) sites on the internet that promise to get you more followers if you provide them with your username and password. After signing up these sites send spam from your account. **Don't use them**. Buying followers is also against Twitters terms of use and will result in your account being suspended or permanently blocked. I'll cover more about following rules and limits in a minute. First lets look at some of the ways you can grow your following organically:

- Optimise your profile and "Bio" so that it attracts followers in your niche.

- Tweet often. More tweets generally means more followers.

- Use hashtags. This will put your tweets in front of the right people and expand your reach.

- Schedule and automate tweets with tools like Hootsuite

and SocialOomph (more about these and other useful apps in chapter 14). This allows you to be consistent in your posting even when you can't tweet in real time.

- Follow the right people. Find people in your niche or industry to follow, especially those who have a substantial number of followers on Twitter.

- Join in Twitter chats and get involved in conversations. Be actively social.

- Retweet others content.

- Tweet content that will appeal to your target audience.

- Embed tweets.

- Promote your Twitter account everywhere you can.

Following rules and limits.

Earlier I pointed out the importance of growing your following organically and not buying followers. This is just one of Twitters rules. You can find a full list of rules here https://support.twitter.com/articles/18311-the-twitter-rules but in this section I'm going to cover those related to building your following and the limits given by Twitter.

- You are not allowed to use any site that offers to automatically add followers to your account.

- Following and/or unfollowing large amounts of users in

a short time period, particularly by automated means is seen as aggressive following and could land you in trouble.

- Repeatedly following and unfollowing people, regardless of whether it's to build followers or to garner more attention for your profile is frowned upon.

- Do not send large numbers of duplicate @replies or mentions. Large numbers of unsolicited @replies or mentions are seen as an aggressive attempt to bring attention to your product, service, or link.

- Do not add a large number of unrelated users to lists in an attempt to bring attention to an account. It will only take away from your author brand.

- Do not create multiple accounts in order to gain followers. Following yourself is just pointless.

What are the limits?

Twitter isn't like the other social media sites. Following someone on Twitter doesn't mean they have to follow you back. Twitter allows people to opt-in, or opt-out, of receiving a persons updates without requiring a mutual relationship. There are some limits though.

Every user can follow 2000 people. Once you've followed 2000 users, Twitter limits come into play and restrict the number of people you can follow. The limit is different for every user and is based of your ratio of followers to following.

When you hit this limit, Twitter will tell you by showing an error message in your browser. You'll need to wait until you have more followers in order to follow more users—for example, you can't follow 10,000 people if only 100 people follow you.

Here's what Twitter says about their limits and best following practices:

"We don't limit the number of followers you can have. However, **we do monitor how aggressively users follow other users**. *We try to make sure that none of our limits restrain reasonable usage, and will not affect most Twitter users.*

We monitor all accounts for aggressive following and follow churn (repeatedly following and un-following large numbers of other users). You can read more about these here, but if you don't follow or un-follow hundreds of users in a single day, and you aren't using automated methods of following users, you should be fine.

Please note that Twitter does not permit any automated or bulk following or un-following behavior.

Limits improve site performance by ensuring that when we send a person's message to all of their followers, the sending of that message is meaningful. Follow limits cannot be lifted by Twitter, and everyone is subject to them, including verified and developer accounts. Based on current behavior in the Twitter community, we've concluded that this is both fair and reasonable."

Whilst growing your following is important, Twitter isn't a race to get the most followers. You need to think long term. Following users that you're interested in and that post interesting content, makes it much more likely that legitimate users will find you and read your updates. People follow other users on Twitter to read updates that are interesting to them so make sure you're putting out content for your target audience and those people will follow you.

Creating your network: Chapter 6

Who to follow

" On Twitter we get excited if someone follows us. In real life we get scared and run away."

Unknown

Shaping your Twitter experience

Now we've covered how to get people to follow you let's take a look at who you should follow. It's hopefully clear by now that finding the right people to follow is fundamental in shaping your Twitter experience and ultimately what you get out of the site. Expose yourself to the right set of influencers and fill your Twitter stream with relevant, interesting content.

Who to follow

As an author there are various groups of people you will want to follow on Twitter. Some examples include:

- **Influencers.** These are the top players in your niche with large followings of their own.

- **Fellow authors.** Whether supporting each other or just to keep tabs on what your competition is doing, following fellow authors is a must.

- **Book bloggers.** These are people who post about books on their blogs and often host authors for interviews and guest posts. They are also likely to post reviews of books to their sites and so are valuable resources to have in your network.

- **Publishers.** If you plan to go the traditional publishing route following publishers is a great way to see what they are doing to promote their authors and check out if they could be a good fit for your own books. It also means you can keep up with when they are open to new submissions. Following publishers is a good idea for self publishers too. You get to see how they are doing things and can get ideas for how you can be professional in marketing your own books.

- **Agents.** Agents know what publishers are looking for and have their finger on the pulse when it comes to industry trends. They are therefore well worth following.

- **Industry news.** Following these profiles will keep you up to date with what's happening in the industry and help you make informed decisions for your books and marketing strategies.

- **Illustrators and graphic designers.** There may come a point when you need a book cover designer, interior book designers or, in the case of children's authors, full illustration services.

- **Book marketing experts.** All authors need to do some marketing regardless of how they are published. Following these people will give you a supply of information and ideas you can apply to your own books and show you ways to get more leverage from your marketing efforts.

- **Avid readers.** Bookworms that tweet about the books they read. These people are one of the main reasons you're using social media in the first place. They read books, write reviews, and share about their favourite authors. These are your potential customers.

This is just the tip of the iceberg and I'm sure you can come up with plenty more. This list is just to give you an idea of the sorts of people you should be looking to follow on Twitter and why.

Directories

One way to find people to follow is to search directories (make sure you list yourself too). These are basically lists of Twitter accounts divided into categories. Directories are great for connecting with new people but also for building targeted awareness for your author brand.

Here's a list of directories you might want to check out:

Who To Follow

- http://booktradedirectory.com/

- http://connect.me/

- http://justtweetit.com/

- http://wefollow.com/

- http://twittercounter.com/

- http://twellow.com/

- http://www.twibs.com/

- http://www.tweetfind.com/

- http://www.twibes.com/

- http://twiends.com/

- http://twitaholic.com/

- http://www.ibegin.com/twitter/

- http://www.localtweeps.com/

- http://twitterpacks.pbworks.com/w/page/22555521/FrontPage

- http://twopcharts.com/

Creating your network: Chapter 7

Lists

" Twitter lists are essential at helping you stay engaged with your most important people- especially as you grow into the thousands of followers."

@RivkaK

Building lists

To create a list go to your "lists" page. This can be done by clicking on the gear icon at the top right in your navigation bar or by going to your profile page and clicking on "lists".

Once there click "Create list" and enter the name of your list with a short description of what the list is about. You then selection if you want the list to be private (only you can see it) or public (anyone can subscribe to the list). Finally, click "save list". You're now ready to add people to your list.

Lists

To add someone to your list click on the gear icon on the users profile and select "Add or remove from lists". You don't need to be following a user to be able to add them to a list. A pop up window will appear showing the lists you've created. Tick the box next to the lists you would like to add that user to. That person will now show in the list of members for that list.

Lists you have created and lists by others that you have subscribed to are shown under "subscribed to".

Subscribed to   Member of

Book tweeters

profiles that tweet when you have book deals

31 members

Influencers 🔒

Influencers I want to connect more with

7 members

PD14 Presenters 🔒

14 members

PD13 presenters 🔒

8 members

PiBoIdMo

55 members

To see what lists you're on click on "member of"

Lists

To view tweets from a list just click on the "lists" tab and then on the list you'd like to view. You'll then see a timeline of tweets from users included in that list.

Following lists

Not got time to create your own lists? Simply find relevant lists that have been created by others and follow them.

To subscribe to someone else's lists click on the users profile and then on "lists". This will show you all the lists created by that person. From this page you can click "subscribe" to follow the list. You don't need to be following the person to be able to subscribe to their list.

A few lists you might want to consider following:

- https://twitter.com/jolinsdell/lists/piboidmo

- https://twitter.com/jolinsdell/lists/authors

- https://twitter.com/WritersDigest/lists/publishers

- https://twitter.com/jolinsdell/lists/writers-resources

- https://twitter.com/CJWrightBooks/lists/full-writers-list

- https://twitter.com/adamjayc/lists/bloggers-and-writers

- https://twitter.com/SergeyMarkov/lists/authors-writers-20

- https://twitter.com/ShortStoryWrite/lists/nanowrimo-ers-2013

- https://twitter.com/TeeBylo/lists/tweetingwriters

- https://twitter.com/MarcyPusey/lists/kidlit

- https://twitter.com/Rogercparker/lists/writing-resources

- https://twitter.com/JFbookman/lists/self-publishing

- https://twitter.com/BookYrNextRead/lists/reviewers-interviewers

- https://twitter.com/janefriedman/lists/best-tweets-for-writers

- https://twitter.com/GalleyCat/lists/best-book-review-feeds

Lists

- https://twitter.com/GailMBaugniet/lists/bloggers-of-book-topics-13

- https://twitter.com/WritingSpirit/lists/writing-faves

- https://twitter.com/RachelJameson/lists/writing-tips

- https://twitter.com/Mike_Stelzner/lists/copywritinggurus

- https://twitter.com/NickThacker/lists/writers

- https://twitter.com/Melissa_Foster/lists/book-promos

Section 4: Tweets

Tweets: Chapter 8

Types of content

"Unless it's something really spectacular, don't tweet me your breakfast, I don't care."

@Busyphilipps25

What to tweet

In this chapter I'll be giving you some ideas for the types of content you can share on Twitter and looking at the benefits of each one. Before we move on to that though there's a few things you should know:

Best Tweets

On the newsfeed you'll notice that some tweets show up as normal size whereas others are shown in a bold, larger font. When a tweet is shown in bold it's Twitters way of telling you that it's one of the more popular tweets e.g. a tweet with a high level of engagement (retweets, replies, or favourites).

Pinned Tweets

In the new design you can now pin a tweet of your choice to the top of your profile page. The tweet will remain at the top of your page until you either unpin it or pin a new one.

To pin a tweet you just need to click on the "..." of your chosen tweet and select "Pin to your profile page".

The tweet will then show at the top of your profile Twitterfeed.

To unpin a tweet just click on the "..." and select "unpin from profile page".

Pinned Tweet

Jo Linsdell @jolinsdell · Jun 19

Getting ready for the "How to be Twittertastic" #VBT. Can u host me in July? Sign up now at jolinsdell.com/2014/06/sign-u...

You

How to be Twittertastic
Virtual Book Tour
July 2014

How to be
Twittertastic

View more photos and videos

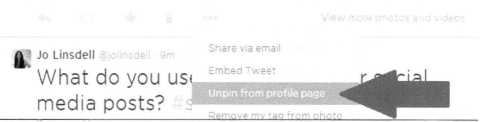

Jo Linsdell @jolinsdell · 9m

What do you us   r   cial
media posts? #s

Share via email

Embed Tweet

Unpin from profile page

Remove my tag from photo

Pinned tweets can be great for getting some extra mileage out of a tweet.

The types of tweets you might want to consider pinning include:

- Important announcements.

- Letting your followers know about an upcoming event.

Types Of Content
- Letting followers know about a special offer.

- Asking a question.

- A call for support e.g. getting people to sign up to be part of your virtual book tour.

- To highlight a great review.

One last thing before we move on... everything you tweet is public. Be careful what you post.

Now lets take a closer look at the types of tweets you can create and the benefits of each one.

Plain text

This is your basic written text tweet using up to 140 characters. Whilst you have up to 140 characters the ideal tweet length is 70-100 characters. This allows space for people to add a comment or tag others when retweeting it.

Here's an example of a text only tweet where the author shares a writing tip:

Retweeted by Jo Linsdell

Jill Pritchett @JillKilihill · Jun 8
#onwriting Hook your reader in the first chapter or, better, the first paragraph. Keep building the tension--conflict creates tension.

Expand   ♻ Retweeted

In this text only example the author shares one of his writing goals:

Fantasy Author @BrianRathbone · Jun 20
Through storytelling I can share my imagination with the world. My goal is to let the reader see the movie that plays in my mind. #amwriting
Expand

This text only tweet shares a quote:

Vikram Narayan @BookBuzzr · 3h
History will be kind to me for I intend to write it. - Winston Churchill #quote
Expand

This one is part of a conversation:

ArtistJMBartz @JaclynMBartz · Jun 17
Thanks for the compliments @johnsdell. I hope you are having a wonderful day! #Appreciated
View conversation

As you can see there are a lot of different types of tweets you can do just using plain text. You'll also probably have noticed that all of the above tweets have something in common. They all contain a hashtag (the # symbol). I'll be covering hashtags in more detail in chapter 12.

Plain text tweets are the easiest and quickest tweets to create whether you're using a computer or a mobile phone to post from.

Types Of Content
Links

As writers you'll probably use this one quite a lot as it allows you to send people to longer blog posts, websites featuring your book, your own website, and, of course, your book sales page. Just tweeting the url isn't going to cut it though.

You'll want to create snappy headline titles to catch the interest of your potential readers and make them want to click the link to read more.

This example clearly shows what the article it links to is about:

Joanna Marple @JoannaMarple · 3h
My Secret for Battling Procrastination janefriedman.com/2011/10/21/sec... **via** @janefriedman

Expand

Instead of just using the title of a link, try pulling a quote from the text to get people interested in what you have to say. If the article is written by someone else, be sure to @ tag them in the tweet to is shows up on the newsfeed of their followers as well.

In this example they quote the question that sparked the article:

Retweeted by Diandra Mae

jennifer laughran @literaticat · 18h
Anonymous author asks: "I've had a big-name agent for some time, but we have problems. Should I stay or should I go?" literaticat.blogspot.com/2014/06/should

Expand

Link tweets can also be used to share about events you're taking part in. This one lets readers know about a writing challenge:

Jarmila V Del Boccio @JarmVee · 14h
I am participating in WOWnonficpic. 7 days, 7 drafts.
kristenfulton.org/official-wow--... kristenfulton.org/wow--nonficpic...
Expand

Why not use someone else's tweet? There are plenty of link tweets being shared so finding one that's on topic with your audience to retweet isn't hard. This one links to a book cover contest:

bookgoodies @bookgoodies · 4m
All book covers are not created equally. If yours is good enter our cover contest.
ow.ly/xRVXN
Expand

We'll be taking a closer look at how and where to find content to share in chapter 15.

Images

They say that "an image is worth a thousand words" and therefore, given that Twitters new design gives more space for visual content, images shouldn't be ignored.

There is also now a specific section in search results for images and videos which just goes to show how important they think visual content is on the site.

59

Types Of Content

A recent study by Dan Zarella showed that images posted using pic.twitter.com (the built in image tweeting feature on Twitter) get 94% more retweets than others. This is also the only way the auto-expand tool works.

In general users respond 40% more often to content with images than they do to plain text content. Visual tweets also make better embedded tweets. I'll cover embedding tweets in chapter 10.

When posting images you can post up to four images on the same tweet. Just click "Add more" (see lower left) to add more photo's.

You can also tag up to 10 people on an image. To tag someone in an image just click on "Who's in this photo?" on the lower right and type their Twitter handle into the tag box when creating the tweet.

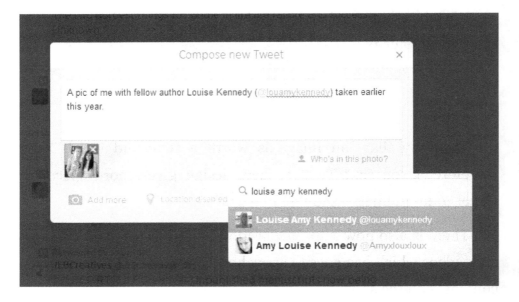

So what kind of images can you tweet?

Here's a few ideas to get you started:

- Photos of you working on your work in progress and other behind the scenes images

- Photos of your writing space/ the view you have from your writing space.

- Photos of your print books.

- Photos from events.

- Photos of you with readers (a great way of giving back to your fans and making them feel special).

- Photos of promotional material and business cards.

- Photos of your book in bookstores.

- Photos of you with other authors.

- An image with a quote written on it (Just take a quote and place it over an image of your choice). As you can see from this example, the "image" doesn't need to be anything special. Even a plain background is enough.

Types Of Content

Claudia Y. Burgoa @yuribeans · 13h
"We are all apprentices in a craft where no one ever becomes a master." —
Ernest Hemingway
#amwriting

> # We are all apprentices in a craft where no one ever becomes a master.
>
> — *Ernest Hemingway*

RETWEETS FAVORITES
21   15

4:23 AM · 22 Jun 2014 · Details   Flag media

Collapse   ↰ Reply ♺ Retweet ★ Favorite ⋯ More

- Screenshots of blogs featuring one of your posts.

- Screenshot of a review on Amazon, Smashwords, or other retail site.

- Screenshot showing your book listed as a best seller on a retail site.

- Promotional banners for your books or special offers.

- Infographics (this could be something like your own top tips for writing a INSERT YOUR NICHE HERE book to help establish yourself as an expert in your field or a step by step of your writing process to show readers how you work).

- GIFs (This is a brand new feature that was launched June 2014. GIFs are animated images on a continuous loop and appear on the timeline with a play button. You can upload GIFs the same way you would upload a regular photo using the gallery button under the text box. Note that although GIFs are uploaded like photos you can only upload one at a time and not four like you can with normal, static photos).

Video

Video is a great medium for connecting with your followers and allows plenty of room for creativity.

You can tweet videos from YouTube and people can then watch them directly from your Twitter feed. A great way to connect the two social media sites.

You can share your own videos or ones created by someone else. In this example I tweeted a funny video about writing that I found on YouTube:

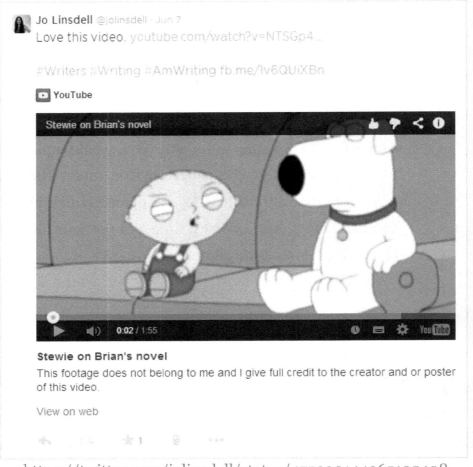

https://twitter.com/jolinsdell/status/475320144265105408

If creating video content for YouTube seems like too much work check out Vine (https://vine.co/). Vine is Twitters official video service and makes sharing video content on the site super quick and easy. In true Twitter form, each vine video lasts 6 seconds or less. Bite-size video content.

So how can you as a writer use Vine? Here's a few ideas:

- Show your favourite writing spot.

- Make a short book trailer.

- Show off your book.

- Review a book.

- Share an inspiring quote.

- Share a line or two from your book/work in progress.

A former Twitter employee started a video series using Vine based on the choose your own adventure books. You can read more about that here http://mashable.com/2014/05/26/choose-your-own-adventure-vine/. Why not let your fans give input into what happens next in your book by using a similar idea. Let them pick from two different scenario's and decide what happens next to your protagonist. A great way of engaging your fans whilst at the same time creating a buzz about your work in progress.

You might also want to try live streaming video to your Twitter feed using a site like www.Twitcam.com. This could work well for question and answer sessions or for sharing quick tips or updates on your current work in progress.

There's no need for special software or even signing up. You just log in with your Twitter account. It's also completely free to use.

Screenshot of the TwitCam website

Chats

Chats are an excellent way to network with others in your industry, and are also great for connecting with readers and reinforcing your author brand.

There are thousands of weekly chats already in place on Twitter that are hosted by others. Just find a few that fit your niche and join in the conversation. Alternatively you can host your own. Each chat has it's own individual hashtag that is used on all the tweets involved in the chat to make them easy to find.

You can also do an author interview in chat format. Again, you'll need a unique hashtag to attach to tweets. Have another tweeter ask you questions or host the interview yourself and ask a fellow author, publisher, etc... some questions.

You could even do an open chat with your fans where they can tweet you their own questions for you to answer.

In order for a chat to run smoothly you need a way of singling out all the tweets relevant to the chat. You can type in the hashtag for the chat in the search bar on Twitter and that will bring up matching tweets. Another way to filter a chat is to use a third party app like www.Tweetchat.com where you sign in with your Twitter account and type in the hashtag you want to follow.

Screenshot from TweetChat

I have a little system that I find works quite well for keeping a balance between types of content. It's the 20% rule. It basically involves posting at least 5 tweets per day. Only one of these tweets will be promotional. The others will be a mixture of helpful, inspirational, social, and fun.

Types Of Content

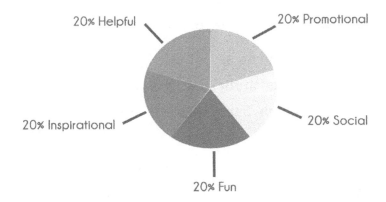

20% Helpful · · · 20% Promotional

20% Inspirational · · · 20% Social

20% Fun

Using this system means that you won't come across as a pushy salesperson. You don't want to spam people. If you want to promote more, just tweet more often. You need to have a balance between self promotion and general value you offer your readers. Answer questions, share quotes, join in conversations, and have fun with some jokes or other fun content.

As you can see there is a lot more to Twitter than just 140 character status updates. The trick is knowing what your followers want to see, and what they are most likely to share with their own friends. A good way of checking if you're on the right track is to ask yourself these questions:

If you saw the tweet, would you want to know more about it?

Would you retweet it?

If your answer is yes, you're probably doing it right.

Tweets: Chapter 9

Tweeting events

"#twitter tips: use location tags when live-tweeting from events so interested parties can find your event"

@museummammy

Be part of the action

Twitter is perfect for connecting and networking more with other attendees during events but also for letting people who can't be there with you know what's happening.

As events are attended by numerous people you have the power of numbers in your favour. Just look at what happened during the Oscars when Ellen took a selfie with some of the stars present. It made Twitter history and became the most viral content on Twitter... ever. The selfie by the Oscar host Ellen DeGeneres is now the most retweeted image of all time and the first to surpass 1 million retweets.

Here's the tweet:

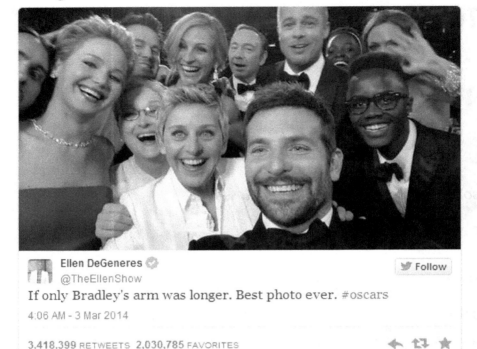

Ellen DeGeneres 🔵
@TheEllenShow

🐦 Follow

If only Bradley's arm was longer. Best photo ever. #oscars

4:06 AM - 3 Mar 2014

3,418,399 RETWEETS 2,030,785 FAVORITES

↩ ⬆ ★

So how do you live tweet an event?

Here's a few things you should do pre-event:

1. Know the hashtag for the event so you can be sure you're using the right one.

2. Research the Twitter handles of speakers/organisers before the event so you can tag them in tweets.

3. Start connecting with other attendees. Reaching out before the actual event will mean you can meet up face to face while you're there and build a stronger bond.

4. Give notice to your followers that you're going to be

posting about a particular event. This allows people who want to engage and follow along to prepare, and the ones that don't will know to check back later.

During the event:

1. Don't try to be everywhere and tweet everything. Pick highlights. If you miss anything out there's a good chance someone else tweeted it. You also don't want to overwhelm your followers with tweets.

2. Offer exclusive content like behind the scenes photos or interviews.

3. Quote speakers and other people at the event using quotation marks and attribute the quote either by using their specific twitter handle or, if you can't find it, identifying them by name.

Promo Day @PromoDayEvent · Jun 1

"the more exposure you get, the more you'll kick in the Amazon algorithms..." Penny Sansevieri (@Bookgal) #PD14 #presentation

Example tweet from the 2014 Promo Day event

4. Don't forget to listen. Other people will be tweeting about the event too. Join in their conversations and retweet

their content too.

Post event:

1. Thank the organisers, speakers, and other attendees.

2. Monitor the hashtag for a few days for follow up comments.

Tweets: Chapter 10

Getting the most out of your tweets

"It's not enough to simply post content on Twitter, you also need to interact with others, Tweet back, #FollowFriday, and thank."

@RickCooper

Be a top Tweeter

Now we've looked at types of content you can create it's time to show you how to get the most out of your tweets. It's not enough to simply tweet.

There's one thing you can do BEFORE you start using Twitter that will help you be a better Tweeter and get you gaining better results from your tweets.

Have a list of goals

What are you hoping to achieve through Twitter? What audience are you hoping to connect with? What kind of content is that audience interested in? By identifying your target audience and your goals you'll be able to build a more solid tweet schedule.

Getting The Most Out Of Your Tweets

Now lets look at best practices you can use to leverage your tweets for maximum effect.

Pinned tweets

This new feature is a great way to single out a specific tweet for your followers. It shows at the top of your profile page meaning that it will be the first tweet people see when they visit your profile.

Embedded tweets

Embedding tweets means you can gain traffic to your tweet (and Twitter profile) from other sites. As embedded tweets are interactive it means people don't need to log into Twitter to be able to view, or engage with it. They can retweet, add to their favourites, and even follow you right from the embedded tweet.

To embed a tweet on your website or blog click "embed this tweet" and select the HTML, shortcode, or link from the pop-up box. Then you just copy and paste the code provided into your blog or website.

Step 1:

Step 2:

Share the direct url for a tweet

Not interactive like embedded tweets but still good for driving traffic from elsewhere to a specific tweet. To find the direct url for a tweet click on the timestamp of the tweet. It will then open up on a page of its own. Copy the url from that page and paste where ever you want.

In addition to these techniques there are things you can do to your tweets to increase the amount of visibility your tweets get.

Be helpful

Be helpful to people you look up to and kind to those who look up to you. Whatever you write about you can probably find the top names in your niche on Twitter and reach them directly. Being a regular, helpful presence will help get you noticed by those people.

Keep tweets short

Tweets of 100 characters or less allow space for people to RT and comment.

It's not all about you

Don't just promote yourself. Be social, be helpful, and share useful content.

Use lists

Clear the clutter and sort tweeters into groups. This will help keep you on topic when connecting and retweeting. By adding yourself to public lists you can group yourself with key players in your topic areas and build your reputation as an expert in your niche.

Stay on topic

Stick to tweeting about what you know best, using your keywords, and you'll soon stand out as an expert in your niche.

Use hashtags

Help your tweet reach the right people by adding hashtags.

Share the love

Take part in shout out events like Writers Wednesday (#WW) and Follow Friday (#FF).

Tweets: Chapter 11

Retweets

"Be an interested tweeter. Comment & RT on follower's posts. Twitter is a conversation, not a broadcast booth."

@marieleslie

Viral content

In this chapter I'll cover retweets and share some tips for getting more of them.

Retweeting other people's content is a great way of reaching out to new followers, connecting with influencers, and having a consistent Twitter presence without too much work involved. It's easy content.

Another good thing about retweets is that they are good for karma. People who retweet other's content tend to get more retweets themselves.

Tweet at the right times.

There is no one-size-fits-all solution for this despite what some "experts" will tell you. You need to find out the best times for YOU. A great tool to use for this is www.tweriod.com. It finds the best times to tweet based on when you and your followers are online.

Ask for a retweet.

Seems simple enough but you'd be surprise at how many people overlook this obvious method. Let people know you want them to retweet your tweet. A few known effective calls to action for retweets include putting "Please retweet", " Pls RT" or "RT" on your tweet.

Tweet links.

Give people more than the 140 characters by linking to an online resource or article. Make sure you include a killer headline or catchy quote from the post to grab their interest and make them want to click the link to read more.

Use keywords.

Find out what the most retweeted words are in your niche and use them in your tweets. In general tweets including words like "how to", "top", "free", "help", and "blog post" tend to do well.

Leave room for retweets.

Try to keep your tweets under 100 characters to leave space for people to add their own comment or tag someone on it. If they need to edit your tweet before they can retweet it they're less likely to retweet it.

Use hashtags.

Hashtags help put your tweet in front of the right audience and therefore help increase your chances of being retweeted. I'll be covering hashtags in more detail in the next chapter.

Quotes.

Quotes are the most viral content. Find or create your own quotes related to your audience and you're almost guaranteed some retweets.

Get visual.

Include an image in your tweet. Social management tool, Buffer, found that their tweets with images contained 18% more retweets and 39% more favorites than those without.

Quality content.

Don't just tweet about yourself. Tweet information, quotes, tips, etc... that are of interest to your followers. Make it about them.

Tweets: Chapter 12

Hashtags

"Don't overuse hashtags in your tweets. Remember, hashtags are meant to help categorise tweets"

@EdmundSLee

Use hashtags... the RIGHT way

Hashtags are used for categorisation on social media and are formed using the pound sign (#) followed by a keyword. An excellent tool for getting your tweets to show up in search and therefore, for putting them in front of the right people.

You do need to be using them the right way though. This YouTube video by Jimmy Fallon and Justin Timberlake shows how some people are getting it wrong. (It's also pretty funny ;)).

Hashtags

https://www.youtube.com/watch?v=57dzaMaouXA

So what is the RIGHT way?

As hashtags are used to highlight keywords and categorise your tweets you need to think about the keywords related to the content you are sharing.

As your main goal is to build your author brand and sell more books you need to think of keywords related to your niche and topic of your book. For example, as this book is about Twitter I use #Twitter and #Twittertastic (both are already used on Twitter but tie in nicely with the topic of the book and link to the book title). I also use #Writers, #Authors, and #SocialMedia as the book is part of the Writers and Authors Guide to Social Media series.

I'll be sharing a list of general hashtags for authors later on in this chapter but for now try to think of a handful of keywords that relate to the topic of your book. As you hopefully included some keywords in your book description this shouldn't be too hard to do.

Be an expert

Hashtags can be a great way to mark yourself as an expert in your field. Single in on related hashtags that narrow down what most of your content will be about in the long term. This will mean that your tweets start coming up regularly in searches for your niche.

Consider branding your own hashtag

Whilst there are plenty of hashtags out there that you can hop on, you can also create your own to further strengthen your brand. Try to come up with a personal hashtag to be used on posts about your book. This will make it easier for you to find out when people are tweeting about your book and keep up with feedback and comments.

Hashtags for writers and authors:

Books and Reading Hashtags

#Books
#BookWorm
#GreatReads

Hashtags
#IndieThursday

#MustRead

#Novel

#Paperbacks

#Storytelling

#WhatToRead

Book Industry News and Publishing Tips Hashtags

#AskAgent

#AskAuthor

#AskEditor

#BookMarket

#BookMarketing

#GetPublished

#IAN1 (Independent Author Network)

#IndiePub

#PromoTip

#Publishing

#SelfPublishing

#WriteTip

#WritingTip

Hashtags to Connect With Other Writers

#1K1H (write one thousand words in one hour)

#AmWriting

#AmEditing

#AmRevising

#CopyWriting

#EditGoal

#Editing

#IndieAuthor

#MyWANA (writer's community created by Kirsten Lamb)

#NaNoWriMo (National Novel Writing Month- held every November)

#RomanceWriter

#ScriptChat

#WIP (work in progress)

#WordCount

#WriteChat

#WriteGoal

#WriteMotivation

#WritersLIfe

#WriterWednesday

#Writing

#WritingBlitz

#WritingPrompt

#WritersBlock

#WroteToday

#WW

#StoryStarter

Hashtags
#WordAThon

#Creativity

ePublishing and eBooks

#Amazon

#eBook

#BookBuzzr

#eReaders

#ePubChat

#iPad

#Kindle

#KindleBargain

#Kobo

#KDP (Kindle Direct Publishing)

#Nook

#Pubit

#SmashWords

#Sony

#Webfic

Genre and Specialty Hashtags

#140Poem

#Crime

#Comedy

#DarkFantasy

#Dystopian

#Erotica

#HistFic

#Historical

#FaithLitChat

#KidLitChat

#KidLit

#Literature

#LitFic

#MemoirChat

#MGLit (middle grade literature)

#Mystery

#NonFiction

#Paranormal

#Poetry

#PoetryMonth (Each April in the USA)

#Romantic

#RomanticSuspense

#TrueStories

#ScienceFiction

#SciFiChat

#ShortStory

#SteamPunk

#Suspense

#UrbanFantasy

#WomensFiction

Hashtags
#YA

#YALit

Promotion, Networking and Marketing Hashtags

#99c (to offer or pick up an eBook bargain)

#AuthorRT

#BookGiveaway

#BookMarketing

#FollowFriday

#FreebieFriday

#FreeReads

#Novelines (to quote your own work)

Mobile: Chapter 13

Tweeting on the go

"It's hard to resist tweeting about my new book when I'm on the go, so I often pull to the curb to do it when a brilliant blurb comes to me!"

@FrugalBookPromo

Go mobile

In this chapter I'll give an overview of mobile Twitter and how it works.

Mobile is written into the DNA of Twitter. Twitter leads itself to real-time marketing more than any other social media site. Built around the idea of SMS text messaging, Twitter was made for mobile. According to Search Engine Journal, 71% of users access social media from a mobile device and a recent study by Nielson stated that a huge 80% of UK users access Twitter via a mobile device.

You can sign up for mobile Twitter at https://mobile.twitter.com/ and use it on any device. As with the

Tweeting On The Go
actual website, mobile Twitter is completely free to use.

Accessing mobile.twitter.com on a smartphone or tablet.

All you have to do to access Twitters mobile website is point your
smartphone or tablet browser to mobile.twitter.com. On the
welcome screen, you have the option to sign up for a new account or
sign in with an existing account.

If you have already created a Twitter account just sign in with
your log in details.

If you're new to Twitter click on the sign up button and fill in
your details of your account (name, username, email address, and
password), and click the "create my account" button. You'll then
receive an email confirmation containing a link to click to activate
your Twitter account.

Now lets take a look at how the mobile site works.

Composing a tweet.

Enter your 140 character message in the status update box and
click "tweet". Once you have tweeted your message, your tweet with
be posted to your Twitter profile and in the home timeline of your
followers.

You can also add photos or videos by clicking on the camera
icon and either take a photo or select an existing one to include in

your tweet.

How to follow.

You have two ways to follow users on Twitter.

1. From a users tweet.

2. From the users profile.

In both cases, just tap the follow button to follow the user. To unfollow them just tap the same button again.

Navigation.

The main parts of the site are "Home", which is where you see tweets from accounts you follow, and "#Discover", which is where you can see the latest top tweets and trending tweets.

From the home timeline you can click on an individual Tweet to see the tweets details page. From there you can reply to, retweet, quote, or mark the Tweet as a favourite.

There is also a notification tab where you can see interactions. (who has retweeted you, followed you, mentioned you, and marked your tweets as favourites).

At the top of your screen you'll find the search bar. Here you can search for other users, keywords, hashtags, etc...

Section 7: Useful resources

Useful resources: Chapter 14

Time savers and apps

"#twitter tips: #AuthorsUse a free tool called bitly to shorten any weblinks in your bio, and track click throughs"

@tweetauthors

Twitter tools and applications

There are hundreds of websites, tools, and applications available online that you can use to help you create, schedule, monitor, and filter Twitter content. In this chapter I'll cover some you may want to check out.

Creating images

These are resources you can use to quickly and easily create visual content to share on Twitter.

- http://pixlr.com/

- http://piktochart.com/

- https://www.canva.com/

- http://picmonkey.com/

- http://quozio.com/index.aspx

Time Savers And Apps

- http://www.fotor.com/

- http://www.internetmarketingninjas.com/seo-tools/favicon-generator-crop-images/

- http://www.photovisi.com/

- http://www.befunky.com/

- http://www.easel.ly/

- http://infogr.am/

- http://visual.ly/

- http://www.recitethis.com/

- http://www.pinwords.com/

- http://pinstamatic.com/

- http://www.autreplanete.com/ap-social-media-image-maker/

- http://www.techsmith.com/snagit.html

Scheduling and filtering

These are tools that allow you to schedule posts in advance and help you filter your Twitter content.

- http://tweetdeck.com/

- http://socialoomph.com/

- http://hootsuite.com/

- http://bufferapp.com/

- http://cotweet.com/

- http://twitterfeed.com/

- http://www.mytweetplace.com/

- http://manageflitter.com/

- https://dlvr.it/

- http://twuffer.com/

- http://laterbro.com/

- http://www.twaitter.com/

- http://futuretweets.com/

- http://www.dynamictweets.com/

- http://sproutsocial.com/

- http://www.tweetings.net/

- http://destroytoday.com/work/destroytwitter/

- http://www.sobees.com/

- http://www.tweetadder.com/

Misc

Here I've listed those that don't fit into the above categories.

Time Savers And Apps

- http://paper.li/

- http://bitly.com/

- http://triberr.com/

- http://twitstamp.com/

- http://www.twitbin.com/

- http://clicktotweet.com/

- http://twitcam.com/

- https://storify.com/

- http://tweetreach.com/

- http://www.tweetails.com/

- http://tweriod.com/

Useful resources: Chapter 15

Finding content

"If you are sharing someone's blog, add their @ to the tweet to help your twitter account be found"

@SimpleTurtles

On Twitter

You can easily find a wide variety of content directly on Twitter. One way is using filtered tweets. This feature allows you to filter tweets you see on your page, and anyone else's page you're looking at. This makes it quick and easy to sort through tweets. You can filter just a users tweets, their tweets with @replies, or only the tweets where they've embedded photos or videos.

Another way is by using search. In the search bar at the top right of the site you can type hashtags, keywords, names of people or usernames and Twitter will find all tweets/profiles that fit your search specifics. You can even select whether you want to see just photos and videos or all tweets.

Finding Content
Off Twitter

The internet is full of great content to share. Places to look for content to share are everywhere.

Look at your email subscriptions and blogs you follow. One way to keep track of your subscriptions is to use https://unroll.me/. It allows you to combine your favourite subscriptions into one email making it easier to find content and declutters your inbox at the same time.

http://www.reddit.com/subreddits/ categorizes posts into single focussed lists and covers just about any topic your can imagine.

Find articles online and save them to read later using https://getpocket.com/ The app will also notify you of what's popular and trending.

http://topsy.com/ allows to you search tweets and web content. It even lets you break it down into photos and videos.

Another great site for finding content based on category is http://alltop.com/. Lets not forget our pal https://www.google.com, and with it https://www.youtube.com/ for video content.

I could go on forever here as there are so many sites and apps that pull together content making it easy to find stuff that fits your key topics so I'll stop here but hopefully I've given you some ideas.

Useful resources: Chapter 16

Tweeters that support authors

"Don't aim for followers - work at connections #Twitter tips #Smm"

@GlenGilmore

Supporters

In this chapter I've listed Twitter accounts that specialise in supporting authors.

ReadingDeals.com @Reading_Deals
READERS: Get free and bargain ebooks every day right in your e-mail! AUTHORS: Promote your bargain or free book with our site!

eBook Tweeters @eBookTweeters
There's thousands & thousands of ebooks. We help you find the great ones! AUTHORS: We love you! Follow us and you will be notified when we offer tweet services!

Book Tweeters @TheBookTweeters
READERS: We'll tweet great books for you to read! AUTHORS: Tweet your book to us mentioning @TheBookTweeters and we may RT for you! It's that easy!

Tweeters That Support Authors

eBook Price Drops @eBookPriceDrop
We tweet when books are bargain priced! Don't miss these discounted books! These price drops and ebook deals don't last long!

eBooks We Love @eBooksWeLove
We will be featuring ebooks that should be shared with the world! Want to be notified? Just follow us on here and we will tweet about various books!

eBooks GROW ON TREES @eBooksGOT
We help #authors advertise their FREE & eBook DEALS & #readers discover new reads!
FB:http://on.fb.me/1ccS7Ox Goodreads:http://bit.ly/1djqjLN #kindle

Author Directory @TheAuthorList_
The A List - Promoting Published Authors from All Over the World. NEW LOOK for our website JUNE 1st! Sign UP for our Drawing by 6/30!

BookBear @BookBearFiction
Fall in love with the best of free and discounted eBooks, eBook news, quotes and reviews

SelfPubShowcase @SelfPubShowcase
Showcasing and promoting self-published and small press-published authors from all genres. Helping readers find their new favorite author.

kindleguyz @kindleguyz
Readers: Find the best bargain and free books here | Authors, submit your books at http://bit.ly/17uboel

Author Alliance @AuthorAlliance
#AuthorAlliance is where #Authors, #Publishers &#Readers come together. We promote great #booksin for readers'

delight. #reviews #interviews#promotion

Indie Book Promos @PromoMasq
We promote Indie Authors.

Indie Book Reviews @MasqRev
Book Reviews (featuring the Masq Scale), Author Promotion, Syndication, and so much more.

Indie Book Bargains @IndieBookBargs
Daily UK-based indie book bargains.

Goodkindles @Goodkindles
Great kindle books every day!

KindleBookPromos @freebookpromos
Promoting Kindle deals, authors and free ebook promotions. List your books, promotions and author interviews with us:http://kindlebookpromos.luckycinda.com/

Indie Books @IndBk
Tweeting about Indie books. Got a favorite?

Dot @eReaderBlast
Kindle deals, bargains, and finds! Authors, tweet Kindle title, genre, & http://Amazon.com link @ us for RT! Note: we don't check DMs. New website up soon!

Free Book Dude @FreeBookDude
@FreeBookDude brings you two #FreeKindleBooksevery hour & #FeaturedBook posts from#IndieAuthors. #ShareTheFree

Book Your Next Read @BookYrNextRead
#Bookworm and keen supporter of #IndieAuthorsHere to spread the good word about great #BooksPlease include the hashtag #BYNR We #followback &#RT

Tweeters That Support Authors

Indie Author News @IndieAuthorNews
IndieAuthorNews...where Readers discover Amazing Authors, Book
Features, Hot New Releases, FREE eBooks, Author Interviews,
Book Promotionhttp://t.co/Bm1pITAkeq

Freebooksy @Freebooksy
We find the best free ebooks for Kindle, Nook & Apple. Authors - we
help you connect to readers and sell more books.

AUTHORSdB @AUTHORSdB
The 'Official' Authors Database. Get Listed Today! FREE Publicity.
NEW Book Showcase. We follow back authors only.

iAuthor @i_Author
An interactive advertising platform for authors and
publishers: http://www.iauthor.uk.com. An agile startup, launched
in July 2013, featured on VentureBeat.

Indie_Kindle @IndieKindle
We promote authors--Indie style! Let us Tweet your book--FREE!
List ur books! We'll promote you! Readers, follow us to discover
awesome reads!#IndieKindle

eBook Daily Deals @eBookDailyDeals
eBook Daily Deals, Bargains, and Bestsellers with free previews.
Like us here too:http://www.facebook.com/ebookdailydeal

Kindle Book Review @Kindlbookreview
The Kindle Book Review is a Filter for Kindle Owners to Help Them
Find #Excellent #Kindle #Books.

Anthony Wessel @DigitalBkToday
Helping Readers Find Authors in a Digital World. Kindle books that
are either free, low priced, bestsellers or GOOD READS
recommended by former booksellers.

Book Promotion @book_tribe

Authors, Writers - Get Promotion For Your Books. Readers find great new books to read.http://askdavid.com/book-promotion

Book Chat @BookChat_
#BookReview #Book #Review #Author #GreatReads#Writers #Writing #Quote #Scifi #Romance #Reading#Education #Library #Kindle #Promotion

Retweets for Writers @Retweets4Writer
I only retweet now. When I used to post quotes, my account name was Quotes4Writers but not anymore. See @_WritingQuotes_ for my other Twitter account.

Useful resources: Chapter 17

Learning the lingo

"You can be professional while also 'keeping it real' with your customers. By interacting with customers in a less formal way, you'll build a strong human connection that helps build brand loyalty. "

@Grasshopper

Terminology

Throughout this book I've used Twitter terminology and explained some of them in more detail. I thought it would be a good idea though to give you a summary of Twitter terminology all in the one place for easy reference.

@

The @ symbol is used to single out usernames in tweets. When you use the @ sign followed by a username, it becomes a link to that Twitter profile.

Activity.

Activity is the real-time dashboard where you can view what the people you follow are up to on Twitter.

Algorithm.

An algorithm is a step by step procedure used for calculation. On Twitter it's used to determine most popular tweets and trends.

API.

API stands for Application Programming Interface. It contains all Twitter data and is used to build applications that access Twitter.

Avatar.

Also referred to as your profile photo. This is the photo that represents you on Twitter and shows on your profile and next to all tweets you post to the site.

Bio.

This is a personal description that defines who you are on Twitter. It can be up to a total of 160 characters in length.

Blocking.

This is a feature that allows you to block a person on Twitter. Blocked users can not follow your profile, add you to lists, or tag you in photo's.

Deactivation.

This is when you remove your profile from Twitter. Information from deactivated profiles remains on the system for 30 days.

Developers.

These are engineers who don't work for Twitter but use

Twitter's open source API to build third party applications.

Direct Message.

Also known as DM's, direct messages are private messages between a sender and recipient.

Discover.

The Discover tab is where you can find top tweets, Who to Follow, Activity, Find friends, and Browse categories. It's all about discovering things on Twitter.

Follow.

To follow someone on Twitter is to subscribe to their tweets.

Follow Friday.

Follow Friday is when Twitter users suggest tweeters others should follow by tweeting with the hashtag #FF on Fridays.

Follower.

A follower is another Twitter user who follows your tweets.

Geotagging.

This is tweeting with your location to show where you are in real time.

Hashtag.

The # symbol used to mark keywords and topics.

Lists.

Learning The Lingo

Used to create groups of Twitter users.

Memberships.

These are lists that your profile is included in. You can find them by going to "lists" and clicking on "member of".

Mention.

This is a tweet where your username is used. You are mentioned by another in their tweet/ mention another user in your tweet by including the @ sign followed by their username.

Notifications.

The Notifications tab lets you view interactions, mentions, recent followers, retweets, and see who has favourited your tweets.

OAuth.

This is a method used to grant a third party access to your account without giving them your password.

Profile.

This is a page displaying information about a user and shows all the tweets they have posted.

Promoted Tweets.

These are tweets by people who have paid to promote them at the top of search results on Twitter.

Reply.

A reply always beings with @username and in usually posted by clicking the "reply" button next to a tweet in your timeline. You are replying to another users tweet.

Retweet.

Used to share tweets on Twitter. The act of forwarding another persons tweet to all of your followers. The abbreviated version is RT.

Third party application.

This is a product created by a company other than Twitter that's used to access Twitter data.

Timeline.

A real-time list of tweets on Twitter.

Timestamp.

This is when a tweet was posted to Twitter. It can be found in grey text directly below any tweet. It is also a link to the url for that specific tweet.

Trends.

A subject that is, according to the algorithm, determined to be one of the most popular on Twitter at the moment.

Tweet.

A message posted on Twitter containing 140 characters or less.

Twitter handle

This is the username selected by a user.

Section 9: Final thoughts

Final thoughts: Chapter 18

Conclusion

"Don't tweet all about you: tweet about them"

@buffer

Time to be Twittertastic!

Now it's time to put all the information in this book into action. In this book I've laid out the how to of Twitter and given you tips and strategies to leverage your Twitter presence for best results. You are now ready to be Twittertastic! As I've covered a lot of information over the duration of this book I thought it would be a good idea to summarise the main points here into a step by step check list.

1. Think about SEO and use keywords when creating your account.

2. Personalise your profile.

3. Let people know you're on Twitter.

4. Know your audience

5. Build your following.

6. Be social.

117

Conclusion

7. Tweet different types of content.

8. Get involved in events.

9. Retweet.

10. Use hashtags (without over doing it).

11. Understand Twitter etiquette and apply it.

12. Go mobile.

13. Be organised and schedule some of your tweets in advance for better coverage whilst saving yourself time.

14. Share other people's content that is relevant to your audience.

15. Reach out to Tweeters who support authors/love books.

16. Take it to the next level by exploring Twitter apps.

17. Learn the lingo.

18. Be consistent.

19. Have fun!

This book is designed to give you all the information you need to be able to set up your Twitter account and get the most out of your tweeting efforts. As with all marketing efforts the results will be different for each person. With this book I hope to have given you a step by step process of what you can do and how to do it, and supplied you with some ideas to get you start

Final thoughts: Chapter 19

Help spread the word!

"#twittertip Don't start your promotions with @... only the person you're tweeting & tweeps who follow u both will see it. "

@Dorset_Vegan

Share your thoughts

Thank you for reading this book. I hope you've found it useful and encourage you to leave a review on Amazon, Goodreads and any other site where reviews are posted. I really appreciate your help!

I also encourage you to share about this book on your social media channels.

Thank you so much for your help and I hope you enjoyed this book.

Also by Jo Linsdell

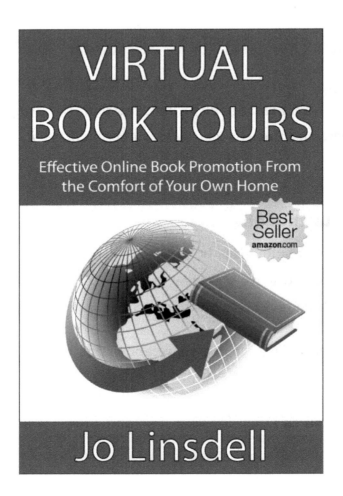

ASIN: B00ELNAQ92

ISBN-10: 1492920932

ISBN-13: 978-1492920939